PRESENTING YOURSELF

HOW TO MAKE A GREAT IMPRESSION

CAREERS WITH EARNING POTENTIAL

CAR MECHANIC

CHEF

COSMETOLOGIST

DOG GROOMER

MASSAGE THERAPIST

FARMER

THE ARTS

———

PRESENTING YOURSELF

PRESENTING YOURSELF

HOW TO MAKE A GREAT IMPRESSION

Mason Crest
450 Parkway Drive, Suite D
Broomall, Pennsylvania 19008
(866) MCP-BOOK (toll-free)
www.masoncrest.com

First printing
9 8 7 6 5 4 3 2 1

ISBN (hardback) 978-1-4222-4328-2
ISBN (series) 978-1-4222-4319-0
ISBN (ebook) 978-1-4222-7492-7

Cataloging in Publication Data on file with the publisher.

Developed and Produced by National Highlights, Inc.
Editor: Andrew Gance
Interior and cover design: Jana Rade, impact studios
Interior layout: Tara Raymo, CreativelyTara
Production: Michelle Luke
Proofreader: Abby Jaworski

NATIONAL
HIGHLIGHTS

KEY ICONS TO LOOK FOR:

 WORDS TO UNDERSTAND: These words with their easy-to-understand definitions will increase the reader's understanding of the text while building vocabulary skills.

 SIDEBARS: This boxed material within the main text allows readers to build knowledge, gain insights, explore possibilities, and broaden their perspectives by weaving together additional information to provide realistic and holistic perspectives.

 EDUCATIONAL VIDEOS: Readers can view videos by scanning our QR codes, providing them with additional educational content to supplement the text. Examples include news coverage, moments in history, speeches, iconic sports moments, and much more!

 TEXT-DEPENDENT QUESTIONS: These questions send the reader back to the text for more careful attention to the evidence presented there.

 RESEARCH PROJECTS: Readers are pointed toward areas of further inquiry connected to each chapter. Suggestions are provided for projects that encourage deeper research and analysis.

 SERIES GLOSSARY OF KEY TERMS: This back-of-the-book glossary contains terminology used throughout this series. Words found here increase the reader's ability to read and comprehend higher-level books and articles in this field.

ambitious: showing strong determination and a desire to succeed

entry-level job: one that requires only basic skills

mentoring: providing guidance and advice to someone who is younger or less experienced

work ethic: always working hard at a job regardless of the task

CHAPTER 1

YOUR FUTURE CAREER

FROM STUDENT TO PROFESSIONAL

One thing is certain in life unless you win big in the lottery: You will graduate from high school and either need to get a job, go to college, or train for a career in some way.

But don't be scared by the fact that you'll have to get a job someday and make your own money and way in the world. This is one of the most exciting times of your life. When you graduate from high school, you'll finally be considered a young adult. You'll have freedom that you could only dream about during those times when your mom and dad told you to clean your room, do your homework, or go to bed at a certain time. You'll get to make your own decisions regarding where you'll live (many high school grads still live at home, so don't get too worried about that yet), what career you'll pursue, and how you'll train for it. There are many ways to prepare for a career, which we'll discuss in this chapter.

TRUE OR FALSE?
ARE YOU READY FOR A CAREER?

1. There are many ways to prepare for a career.
2. Apprentices do not receive pay for their work.
3. Your network can consist of people you know and don't know.

Test yourself as you read. See the end of this chapter for True or False answers.

GOING TO COLLEGE

A college education can be a wonderful thing. Education, no matter where and how you get it, is a valuable tool in life—and college is one of the most exciting and intellectually stimulating places to get an education. There are some careers for which four years of college—or many more than that—are absolutely required for even an entry-level job. You're never going to become a doctor or a lawyer without spending lots of time in college and university classrooms!

Most colleges also offer courses and programs in areas that might not seem directly applicable to a work situation but are important for building a young person's understanding of people, cultures, arts, and sciences, which may not be available to them otherwise. You never know what seemingly unrelated piece of knowledge could trigger your imagination and get you started on the road to success. Steve Jobs, for example, a college dropout and founder of Apple, attributed the inspiration for his innovative designs to a calligraphy (the decorative writing of letters and words) course he took as a young man.

Similarly, college can be the time when young people learn important soft skills, such as cooperation and compromise. Having a roommate, learning to

High school graduates can pursue a wide variety of educational paths to prepare for a career.

interact with your peers on campus, and experiencing mentoring relationships with professors are all life-shaping opportunities.

But the knowledge and skills one learns in college do not always translate to success once a college graduate begins a career. Some skills are learned on the job. Despite this, employers of workers in certain occupations continue to require a college diploma before they will even consider an application. "A college diploma is simply a credential [proof of achievement or qualifications] that at best says you're smart and ambitious," says John Tamny, a political and economics writer, reacting to politicians who insist on the need to see more young people in America graduate from college.

Yet despite the fact that a significant segment of society agrees with Tamny, many people today do see college as the only way to find a stable, well-paying career. This is part of the reason that in 2016, nearly seven out of every ten students in the United States who graduated from high school went on to

Earning a bachelor's degree is a good strategy for some young people, but attending college can be expensive.

attend college, according to the U.S. Department of Labor (USDL). Unfortunately, a college education isn't necessarily a safe bet when it comes to finding a successful career. The *Wall Street Journal* reports that students who graduated from college with debt (money owed to a person, company, or organization) had average debt of $37,712. This much debt takes more than ten years to pay off! Additionally, studies have shown that some university graduates cannot find a job that is a good match for their degree or they can only find jobs that don't require a university degree! This is why a growing number of young people are pursuing other educational paths that prepare them for good jobs.

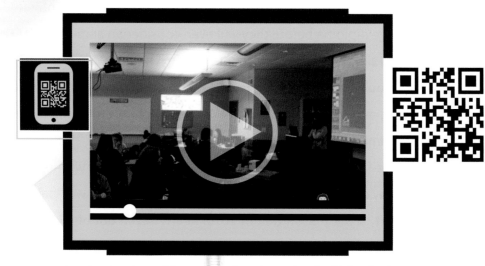

An educator gives advice on choosing what to do after high school.

OTHER EDUCATIONAL AND TRAINING OPTIONS

Many good-paying careers are available for those who do not earn a bachelor's degree (one that requires the completion of four years of college after high school). Nine of the twenty fastest-growing job fields in the United States do not require a four-year college degree, according to the USDL. Quickly growing job fields offer more opportunities for employment, less competition for available positions, fewer layoffs, and, usually, faster and more substantial wage increases than other careers.

Getting one of these jobs, though, doesn't mean you can simply graduate from high school and show up. Almost all careers require some sort of training after high school. Some of the fastest-growing fields—such as physical therapist assistant and occupational therapy assistant—require the completion of an associate's degree, which involves two years of study after high school.

But some of the jobs on the USDL list don't require a degree, and instead, job seekers attend a training program or vocational school, which is a school that trains them for a specific career but has shorter courses of study and is much cheaper than a traditional four-year college. Vocational school programs last from six months to two years. They can be completed on a part-time basis so that students can work in other jobs and support themselves while they acquire new skills.

An apprenticeship is another type of nondegree training program that is popular with students. It is a formal training opportunity that combines classroom instruction and supervised practical experience. Apprentices are paid a salary that increases as they obtain experience. Apprenticeships last

Participating in an apprenticeship is a good option for those who want to earn while they learn.

longer than a vocational school education, typically about four years (although some are shorter), and sometimes require apprentices to take classes at local community colleges (which offer short-term training opportunities and associates degrees). More than 150,000 employers in the United States offer apprenticeships, according to the USDL. Apprenticeships are also available throughout the world.

Some jobs do not require any type of formal training, just on-the-job training. These positions don't typically pay a lot, but they serve as a good way to make money while you train for another career or try to choose an occupational path.

Finally, many people prepare for careers by joining the military. The armed forces offer training in a wide variety of careers—from electronics and health care to law enforcement and cybersecurity.

Before you decide whether or not to go to college, you should do the following things:

- Learn which careers are the fastest growing and the highest paying
- Understand how you can become prepared for these careers and how much time and money this training costs
- Become aware of what kind of work you would like to do and how hard you are willing to work to train for this career

PREPARING YOURSELF FOR THE JOB HUNT

Preparing yourself for the job hunt means many things. In short, looking for a career can be broken down into five actions:

- **Conducting research:** This involves finding out information about fields you might want to work in, companies you might like to work for, salaries you could make, and the careers that are most available to you based on your experiences and location.

- **Developing contacts:** These are people who can help you learn about and research jobs, and they can eventually be useful for recommending you to potential employers. The people you know are your *network*, and meeting new people who might be able to help you find a career is known as *networking*.

Building a good network is key to landing a job. Below, a group of businesspeople network during a break at a conference.

- **Focusing on your skills and training:** You need to develop practical skills that you will use on the job (such as those learned in a vocational school or college), soft skills (communication, leadership, etc.), and job-search skills (such as how to perform well during a job interview).

- **Preparing your résumé:** This key application credential summarizes your experiences and skills that are relevant to the position or career to which you are looking to apply. Preparing a résumé involves not only learning what it should look like and what to include on it but also includes knowing where to post it so that potential employers with open positions will be able to see it.

- **Searching for job openings:** You need to learn where prospective employers post advertisements for open positions and where to look for the careers that would be most suited to you and your experiences.

Reading about and researching these categories (like you are doing now!) is an important step and a great way to prepare yourself for what can be the difficult process of seeking a career. If you have prepared well, not much will surprise you.

Luckily, most of us already have access to a tool that can be very important when it comes to preparing and eventually searching for a career: an internet connection on one's smartphone, computer, tablet, or other electronic device. The internet is a powerful tool for job seekers. Websites such as the USDL's *Occupational Outlook Handbook* (www.bls.gov/ooh) and PayScale.com can be great resources for learning about careers and expected salaries. Many websites offer suggestions or templates (models to copy) for building an attractive and appealing résumé. Others—such as LinkedIn.com and Indeed.com—are great places to post your résumé, learn about companies, build your network, and find job vacancies. Some job seekers even create their own websites that feature their résumé, work samples, photos, videos,

and supportive comments from their current or past bosses and coworkers. You'll still need to learn social skills and how to network, but the internet can help you meet new people, get interviews, and find career counseling centers (places where you can improve your résumé or participate in practice interviews). Learning all the possibilities that the internet has to offer can be an important first step on the road to finding a career.

PRESENTING YOURSELF

No matter how you hunt for jobs—whether by searching on the internet, attending job fairs, or using other methods—you will be, in all instances, expected to treat any contacts or potential employers with a high level of respect. In fact, being respectful to all people (since you never know who can or will be a useful contact) can greatly improve your chances of getting a job. It's also part of being a good person. Your manners, personality, and appearance will show these people that you have respect for them and will allow them to see you in your best possible light. Contacts will be more willing to recommend you to any employers they might know—and employers will be more likely to see the reasons to hire you before they notice any reasons they might not want to hire you. Being able to show others respect through your manners, appearance, and personality is known as "presenting yourself." It can be, above all else, the most important skill for finding a career. Because, after all, who wants to hire someone who is rude and otherwise disrespectful?

All employers, whether they require applicants to have a college degree or not, expect new employees to be hardworking and respectful. Therefore, whether you are applying to be a sales clerk at a local fast food chain or the CEO of a Fortune 500 company, it's your responsibility as an applicant to show a potential employer not only that you are going to work hard for them but also that you take yourself and the position that you are applying for seriously. This is another way to present yourself well.

Whether you're a supermarket clerk or a CEO, it's important that you present yourself professionally.

Presenting yourself in your best possible light may not come naturally. It may mean practicing new skills. It could require taking a look at yourself and improving yourself—your etiquette (customary polite behavior), personal hygiene, personality, and appearance. This doesn't mean that you have to put on a big act or fake who you really are. But you want your "presentation" to represent you and your work ethic.

When employers conduct interviews for a job opening, they generally have a few traits they are looking for in an employee. For example, they may seek a well-organized individual who is able to work successfully as a member of a team. Being organized means keeping work documents and reports in good order, managing your time well, and otherwise structuring your work life so that you can be counted on. Organization is an important quality in most work situations. But if a potential employee walks into an interview late or with a messy briefcase or can't find a copy of their résumé, that tells an interviewer the person was able to organize neither their time nor their personal belongings. You may think it's no big deal to be a few minutes late for an interview—but it could be the detail that makes the employer decide not to hire you.

This may not seem fair. Maybe you just had a bad day. Maybe something came up that was out of your control, something that got you off to a bad start that morning and had you running late. But an interviewer doesn't know that. They have a half hour or so to decide what they think about you. They probably

KEY SKILLS FOR JOB CANDIDATES

In 2018, NACE asked employers to name the soft skills they seek evidence of on candidates' résumés. Here are the most important qualities:

1. Written communication skills: cited by 82.0% of respondents
2. Problem-solving skills: 80.9%
3. Ability to work in a team: 78.7%
4. Initiative: 74.2%
5. Analytical/quantitative skills: 71.9%
6. Strong work ethic: 70.8%
7. Leadership ability: 67.4%
7. Verbal communication skills: 67.4%
9. Detail-oriented personality: 59.6%
9. Technical skills: 59.6%
11. Flexibility/adaptability: 58.4%

have several other applicants to compare you to as well. In a situation like that, details matter!

Nancy R. Mitchell, the founder of The Etiquette Advocate, a firm that provides etiquette training and consulting to large organizations, writes, "Your attitude and behavior toward others are as important as your résumé, experience, training, and technical abilities."

No matter how much experience or how many degrees you have, one thing that can immediately disqualify you for a career is if you present yourself poorly. While factors like the appearance of your résumé are important, businesses, according to Mitchell, "are looking for the human qualities that make the difference in business relationships: courtesy, respect, trust, and reliability [being dependable and doing what you say you will do]. Manners and respect are the

TRUE OR FALSE?
ARE YOU READY FOR A CAREER?

1. There are many ways to prepare for a career.
   True. You can train for a career by going to a two- or four-year college, receiving on-the-job training, joining the military, partici- pating in an apprenticeship, and attending a vocational school.
2. Apprentices do not receive pay for their work.
   False. Apprentices receive pay that increases as they gain expe- rience. For example, an apprentice may start out by earning $12/ hour, and eventually advance to receive $25/hour at the end of their training.
3. Your network can consist of people you know and don't know.
   True. Your personal network consists of family, friends, classmates, and teachers. Your professional network consists of your boss, training director, coworkers, and others you meet at work.

underlying foundation of good relationships, and good relationships translate to business success."

Being able to present yourself well shows that you, as an employee, will represent your employer to the best of your ability. Believe it or not, when it comes to landing your dream job, presenting yourself well could be even more important than whether you decide to go to college!

One component of a strong work ethic is staying late to get the job done.

RESEARCH PROJECT

The following websites will help you match your personality and interests to a good career:

- O*NET OnLine: Skills Search: http://online.onetcenter.org/skills
- The Career Interests Game: https://career.missouri.edu/career-interest-game
- Keirsey Temperament Sorter: www.keirsey.com

What occupations are a good fit? Pick your favorite career and learn more about the educational requirements, job duties, required skills, and employment outlook at www.bls.gov/ooh and other career sites. Write a 250-word report that summarizes your findings.

TEXT-DEPENDENT QUESTIONS

1. What are some training options after high school that do not involve earning a bachelor's degree?
2. What are the five steps to looking for a career?
3. What are the three most important skills hiring managers look for on applicants' résumés, according to NACE?

WORDS TO UNDERSTAND

biased: having unfair favor for or against

elderly: people who are age sixty-five and older

racist: showing bias for or against a person or group based on their race

recruiters: people who search for job candidates for a company

sexist: showing bias for or against a person or group based on their gender

CHAPTER 2

ETIQUETTE, MANNERS, AND COMMUNICATION

GOOD MANNERS, PROPER ETIQUETTE

Etiquette and manners are very similar concepts and practices. Both refer to guidelines for behavior deemed acceptable by a specific group of people or society. They are like laws in that they guide us toward what is considered correct or appropriate behaviors and practices. But unlike laws, no individual or government has been put in charge of enforcing these guidelines. It is up to you, and no one else, to display good manners and proper etiquette!

Etiquette and manners differ in terms of when and why they are used. Manners are general guidelines for behavior that apply to all situations. Examples of good manners include actions that are always appropriate, such as saying "Please" and "Thank you," and general rules such as always treating the elderly

TRUE OR FALSE?
DO YOU HAVE GOOD MANNERS AND ETIQUETTE?

1. It's ok to make off-color jokes at work.
2. Manners and etiquette can vary geographically.
3. It doesn't matter what you post online.

Test yourself as you read. See the end of this chapter for True or False answers.

with respect. Etiquette, on the other hand, refers to guidelines that are specific to a given situation, such as knowing which fork to use during the second course of a dinner or making sure that you begin a formal email with a greeting such as "Dear Ms. Smith." A person might possibly have very good manners while knowing very little about etiquette.

In the business world, understanding the difference between etiquette and manners is important. Good manners are practiced across all cultures, while etiquette tends to vary between cultures. For example, saying "Thank you," listening with respect when someone is talking, and answering when you are spoken to are behaviors that are considered good manners pretty much around the world. On the other hand, a firm and confident handshake is considered good etiquette when initially meeting someone in the United States—but in China, this is not the case. Chinese businesspeople often greet a person by offering a business card that should, according to Chinese etiquette, be graciously accepted and read immediately. And when a Chinese person shakes hands with you, expect the handshake to be softer and last less time than what typically occurs in the West.

Both manners and etiquette demonstrate to employers that you are respectful, considerate, and mature. These are all traits that are valued in any job.

- **Respect** means recognizing other people's value as human beings regardless of their background, race, class, age, gender, or sexuality. It means refusing to do certain things, like laughing at racist or sexist jokes, and that you won't base your opinion of others on unfair and biased assumptions. Respect for others also means you're on time (recognizing that others' time is as important as yours). It means that you dress appropriately for work and you are attentive to others.
- **Consideration** is the act of behaving thoughtfully, showing that you are aware of others' feelings. It means understanding that your actions

It's important to treat your coworkers with respect and kindness regardless of their gender, race, class, age, or sexuality.

have an effect on others and that you are willing to accommodate others' needs. A considerate person offers help where it is needed and appreciates help when it is offered.

- **Maturity** means being able to adjust your behavior for different settings. You don't talk too loudly and distract others in a quiet room where everyone is working; you don't interrupt people when they are talking. You don't laugh or make jokes during a serious moment, and you don't use crude words or tell off-color jokes in the workplace. You pick up on social cues as to what is expected of you; you don't overreact to frustration or get your feelings hurt easily.

These are the foundations for good manners and proper etiquette—and these traits can set you apart from a candidate with similar skills and education. According to company recruiters and hiring managers, manners and proper etiquette among young people entering the job market are poor, at best. So if you work hard to be sure that you have these qualities, you will already have an edge when it comes to competing in the job market. You'll stand out compared to other job seekers.

Some general etiquette guidelines for employment situations include the following:

- **Research each company and position that you apply for.** At the very least, look up the company online and, if possible, understand where the company is headed and what kind of products or services it provides. It looks bad if you don't even know what a company does, its key players, and a bit of its history when you go in for an interview.
- **Examine your writing.** Every time you send out any sort of communication (whether through the mail or email), make sure that it's free of spelling

and grammatical errors. If possible, have someone else look over your letters and résumé to get a fresh pair of eyes on them.

- **Dress appropriately.** Proper dress etiquette for employment situations includes clean and wrinkle-free clothes. For most interviews, you will want to wear formal business attire. Jewelry and hairstyles should be professional and conservative (modest and conventional), and tattoos should be hidden.

- **Be on time.** Punctuality (timeliness) is important because it proves that you are considerate. If you show up to an interview late, you have just wasted some of the interviewer's time. You have already cost the company money before even stepping in the door! This sends a message that you are not a good time manager.

Being frequently late to work is a good way to lose your job.

- **Have an appropriate attitude.** Be enthusiastic about the position that you are applying for or the work that you're doing. This includes being friendly to others and wearing a confident smile. A lack of enthusiasm in an employment situation is probably a sign that you are working in the wrong field!

It is often said that manners and etiquette are the arts of making others feel comfortable—so while etiquette involves some very specific rules, as long as you make an honest attempt at making others feel comfortable, you will, at the very least, be on the right track!

RESPECTFUL COMMUNICATION

You may have noticed that the general employment etiquette rules listed earlier deal in some way with communication. Communication, in the broadest sense of the word, is the sharing or conveying of information between two or more people.

Communication happens many ways—speech, visual signs (appearance, dress, and body language), writing, and behavior—and always involves at least three things: a sender, a message, and a recipient. It is important to remember these three parts because when you are communicating, especially in the case of an employment situation, you need to be aware that a message may not be understood by the receiver in the way you intend.

In the United States, for example, shaking your head up and down means "yes" and shaking it side to side means "no." In parts of the Middle East, it is the other way around. An American in the Middle East might be sending a message that to them means "yes," while a Middle Easterner might receive the meaning as "no." Although the people you interact with in most job situations will probably understand what you mean if you shake or nod your head, they may misunderstand other messages you are sending. For example, many young people text while they are talking with their friends. They mean no disrespect to their friends, who aren't offended (especially since they're probably texting too). But if you text during a job interview, your interviewer is likely to receive the message that you consider your text conversation more important than the interview—even if that wasn't at all the message you meant to send.

Any communication with a prospective employer requires you to be honest, clear, and considerate. A job interview is not the place to express your creativity by wearing a bizarre outfit or

Standing with your arms folded can send a message that you are not open to new ideas.

bursting into song! During communication that is considerate of the receiver, you're always aware of all of the messages you're sending, even when you may not have intended to send a message at all. For example, you may intend the tattoo of a tree on your arm to communicate your love of nature—but it may communicate to a job interviewer a very different message about the sort of person you are.

Body language is another example of communication that takes place in a job interview. If you slouch in your seat, you indicate a lack of respect to the interviewer. If you sit up straight, you communicate both respect and maturity. If you fail to make eye contact with the interviewer, they may think you're not confident or have something to hide.

Respectful communication involves both the content of your message and the way in which it is delivered. The content of your résumé, for example, refers to what experiences you include on it. How this information is conveyed, on the other hand, refers to your résumé's appearance—what font you use, how large your margins are, the kind of paper you use (if you're sending a hard copy). The experiences and credentials (degrees, awards, certifications, etc.) listed on your résumé might be impressive—but if it's difficult to read or looks unprofessional, potential employers are unlikely to read far enough to be wowed by the credentials you've listed.

Respectful communication conveys information thoughtfully, honestly, and considerately. It is at the core of building positive and healthy relationships. You might think that the ability to form relationships has very little to do with getting a job—but the fact is, relationships are at the core of both finding a job and being successful once you have started work.

ETIQUETTE IN OTHER TIMES AND OTHER PARTS OF THE WORLD

Proper etiquette has very few hard-and-fast rules. If we were able to take a ride in a time machine, we would see many different examples of etiquette depending on what time period we were traveling through. For example, during the Middle Ages, it was good etiquette to give a male guest a bath—but in today's world, a guest would be pretty surprised if they arrived to find a bubble bath waiting for them!

Proper etiquette also varies geographically. In the United States, for example, it is considered polite to make eye contact with someone when they are speaking

In the United States, it is considered polite to make eye contact when having a conversation. In other countries, this may be considered rude.

See some examples of surprising business etiquette practices around the world.

to you—but in other countries, it is considered rude to stare someone in the eye while they are talking. In America, it's common to whistle when applauding at a concert—but in other parts of the world, whistling is considered rude, more akin to booing.

If you travel outside your home country, make sure you are aware of what is considered proper etiquette in that country!

DID YOU KNOW?

In 2018, 95 percent of teens aged thirteen to seventeen reported that they had access to a smartphone, and 45 percent said they were online "almost constantly," according to a survey by the Pew Research Center. Eighty-five percent of teens said that they used YouTube, 72 percent used Instagram, 69 percent utilized Snapchat, and 51 percent used Facebook.

Be sure to clean up your social media accounts before applying for a job. Otherwise, you might be surprised to find something that you forgot to delete or that a friend posted that could ruin your chances of getting hired.

PRESENTING YOURSELF ONLINE

The technology that we use to communicate is advancing rapidly, more rapidly perhaps than our manners and etiquette. From the phone to email to social networking sites, all of these have the possibility of factoring into your employment situation.

Most young people today have spent most of their lives using these technologies. This can be beneficial because young people can use them with a lot more confidence than older applicants. Tech skills can even be listed on a résumé for certain jobs because they are becoming more and more useful, for many reasons, for a great number of fields. On the other hand, negative information about you (even if it is long in your past) can be kept on websites.

Make sure that any representation of yourself on a social networking site is something that you wouldn't mind showing your boss!

Compared to technologies that have been around longer—the phone for example—no rules of etiquette are considered universal for social networking sites and other tech tools. But this is all the more reason to make sure that your manners are top-notch. Proper manners, no matter what medium they are being communicated in, will always be noticed. In a world where manners seem to matter less and less, they only become all the more useful, as good manners can make you stand out from the crowd.

TRUE OR FALSE? DO YOU HAVE GOOD MANNERS AND ETIQUETTE?

1. It's ok to make off-color jokes at work.
   False. Making sexist, racist, or any other type of off-color joke at work is a sure way to get fired. Making these types of jokes creates a hostile work environment.
2. Manners and etiquette can vary geographically.
   True. For example, German people as a rule are more formal and structured in business dealings, while for Italians, business is often personal and relationship driven. You may be asked to go out for a cup of coffee or lunch to build a relationship before getting down to business.
3. It doesn't matter what you post online.
   False. Seventy percent of employers surveyed by CareerBuilder in 2018 said that they used social networking sites to research job candidates. Fifty-seven percent of this group found content that caused them not to hire candidates.

RESEARCH PROJECT

Think about interactions you have had recently with your friends, parents, teachers, and employers. How were your manners and etiquette? What did you do wrong and right? Write a one-page list of how you can improve your manners and etiquette, and refer to it every day to become a better person.

TEXT-DEPENDENT QUESTIONS

1. What's the difference between manners and etiquette?
2. Can you provide an example of a difference in body language between two countries?
3. What are two general etiquette guidelines for employment situations?

complement: to enhance or improve

effective: good at getting a result

internship: a paid or unpaid learning opportunity in which a student works at a business for anywhere from a few weeks to a year to obtain experience

irrelevant: not having anything to do with a subject or situation

qualified: having the right skills, knowledge, and experience for a particular job

CHAPTER 3

WRITING A TOP-NOTCH RÉSUMÉ AND COVER LETTER

THE IMPORTANCE OF A STRONG RÉSUMÉ

A résumé is a summary of the experiences and skills relevant to the field of work that you are hoping to enter. It includes an overview of your accomplishments, shows a prospective employer that you are qualified for the work you want to do, and (ideally) demonstrates why you, above all others considered for the job, would be best suited for the particular position you're applying for.

TRUE OR FALSE?
ARE YOU A COVER LETTER AND RÉSUMÉ EXPERT?

1. Job seekers do not use cover letters anymore.
2. A résumé should ideally be one page.
3. You should use as many different fonts and design elements as possible on your résumé so that you will impress the hiring manager with your creativity.

Test yourself as you read. See the end of this chapter for True or False answers.

When it comes to communication, your résumé is often the first thing that you create to communicate with a potential employer. Therefore, learning how to write a clear, effective résumé is perhaps one of the most important steps toward finding a career.

WHAT TO INCLUDE, WHAT NOT TO INCLUDE

Even as a young person, you already have had many experiences, a number of which may seem extremely important to you. What may seem like an important experience to you, however, may not be considered important by a prospective employer! Choosing wisely which of these experiences to include on a résumé informs an employer of only those reasons that they should hire you. It communicates that you understand all the skills you will need to be successful if you're offered the position. Remaining considerate of a potential employer also means you understand that they only want to hear about those experiences of yours that make you a good match for the position. (They're really not interested in hearing about how good you are at computer games or your amazing scuba-diving vacation—unless either of those applies in some way to the job opening.)

Some information should always be included on a résumé, such as your contact information (including your name, address, email address, and phone number) and a few references—people who will speak well of your character,

Don't include your love of college basketball on your résumé or cover letter unless you're applying for a basketball-related job.

skills, or work ethic on your behalf. When it comes to your experiences, all potential employers want to see three kinds of experience listed:

- your work history
- your education
- your relevant skills (including knowledge of software, machines, languages, and/or tools)

Your résumé is a record of your life's accomplishments, so while you want to keep it relevant to the position that you are applying for, it's ok to brag a little. While humility is an admirable trait, it is a very difficult thing to communicate through a résumé. Your prospective employer will assume you listed the most admirable experiences of your life on a résumé, so do not hold back. When you list your work history, for example, list in detail your responsibilities and accomplishments related to your work, especially any accomplishments that exhibit skills relevant to the company and position you are applying for. Try to include hard numbers that show your work at a company or other organization made a difference. If sales increased during your employment, say so (if you played a role in the sales increase). If customer wait times decreased by five minutes while you worked as a customer service manager, put it on your résumé. Present yourself in the best possible light. On the other hand, don't exaggerate your past experiences; for instance, if you were in charge of taking out the trash for an office, don't say you were the office manager!

You may also want to include your hobbies and volunteer activities if they demonstrate something about you that makes you more qualified for a job. A young person who has just entered the job market, for example, would want to include any extracurricular activities that they may have participated in during their time in high school (especially those in which they took a leadership role), any volunteer work they have done, and any internships that they have completed.

On your résumé, try to include hard numbers—such as improvements in sales while you worked at a previous employer.

If you're applying for your first job working in a daycare facility, and you have no formal experience but you've been taking care of your little brother and sister every day after school for their entire lives, make sure your résumé communicates that!

Someone who is older and has more work experience, however, would probably want to stay away from mentioning high school experiences on their résumé, because this communicates to a potential employer that they haven't done much since high school. Your most recent experiences are those that you want to spend the most time describing.

DID YOU KNOW?

According to a 2017 survey by CareerBuilder.com, 39 percent of human resource managers reported that they spent less than a minute initially reviewing a résumé, and 19 percent spent less than thirty seconds.

An important rule to remember when considering what to include on your résumé is that an employer is only interested in those experiences that demonstrate your skills. For example, being the captain of a high school sports team shows that you have leadership skills and an ability to direct others, traits that are highly valued by most employers.

You will probably apply to multiple companies and, sometimes, even entirely different fields at the same time, so you should target your résumé to each employer. This means you need to remove all irrelevant skills and experiences from the list. When applying for a job as an electrician, for example, your experience babysitting may be completely irrelevant to the work you will be doing. Including irrelevant skills and experiences may communicate

Learn six things that every high school student should put on their résumé.

to a prospective employer that you do not fully understand the skills that are required to be successful in a particular position. It can also tell the employer that you are sending your résumé to other companies as well. As an applicant, you always want a potential employer to think you are completely focused on that company. A good way to determine what skills (leadership, organizational, communication, etc.) the employer is seeking is to read the job listing. You can then reference these skills on your résumé and cover letter.

YOUR RÉSUMÉ'S APPEARANCE

Your résumé should stand out from others, but that's no reason to try out fancy new fonts or wild design elements. What may appear attractive to you might look ugly, flashy, or just plain silly to an employer.

Play it safe—but at the same time, remember that employers are busy people who will spend, on average, thirty seconds to a minute looking at a résumé. You want to quickly direct the employer's eye to the most important information. Therefore, your résumé needs to be, if possible, no more than a page long, and it should be clear and easy to read.

Remember: Having good manners and proper etiquette means showing consideration for what a prospective employer expects from you. Your résumé is not the place to demonstrate your originality by listing your credentials in poem form or by scribbling cute little doodles in the margins.

Here are some tips on formatting a résumé:

- Your résumé's format should be consistent. Don't switch fonts mid-line, for example.
- One-inch margins are standard for all pages.
- Font size should be between ten and twelve points. Your name (placed at the top of your résumé) should be slightly larger and bolded.
- Easy-to-read fonts include Times New Roman, Arial, Century, MS Sans Serif, Book Antiqua, Century Gothic, and Calibri.
- An uncluttered document is visually pleasing, so do not make your résumé too crowded. You want lots of empty space on the page, so do not over-describe any experiences.
- Keep your presentation consistent. This means you may want to make all the main headings bold and italicize all your past titles, or something similar.
- If printing and mailing your résumé, do not use cheap paper (it should be at least 25 percent cotton) and only print on white, off-white, or light-gray paper. Do not use colored paper.
- Proofread your résumé carefully. Have someone else review it too. Spelling or grammatical mistakes communicate to an employer that you may be careless, a trait that no employer values!

There are three kinds of résumés: chronological, functional, and a combination of the two. The differences between them only have to do with the order in which you list your experiences.

Chronological means that events are arranged in the order of the time that they occurred. A chronological résumé starts by listing your work history, with the most recent position listed first, and then your education and skills after this. Chronological résumés can be difficult to target. You do not want to leave out any work experiences; however, work experiences that are not relevant to the position you are applying for should not be explained or explained only briefly.

A *functional* résumé is rarely used and highlights only relevant skills, education, and past work experience. Job seekers who are changing careers or did not work for a significant amount of time typically use a functional résumé. A gap in your work history will be very apparent on a chronological résumé. Therefore, a functional résumé can be used to make this gap less apparent and still demonstrate relevant skills.

A combination of the two might be your best bet, especially for a young person, because a *combination résumé* is the easiest to target. A

It's important to choose a résumé format that's a good match for the amount of experience and number of skills you have.

combination résumé lists your skills, education, and relevant experiences first and then your work history after, in chronological order.

RÉSUMÉS FOR CREATIVE CAREERS

The only situation in which you will want to stray from a professional, conservative résumé is when you are applying for an art or design position, especially if the company to which you're applying is very cutting edge. In that case, you want your résumé to showcase your own design skills and creativity—and you want it to stand out from all the other résumés being submitted. You might want to also include some examples of your work on a flash drive or a link to samples of your work online. Your résumé still needs to be clear and readable—it shouldn't be so creative that the busy employer would have to spend more than thirty seconds deciphering it—but expressing yourself through your résumé for a creative job can be a good way to demonstrate what you can offer the employer.

WRITING A COVER LETTER

A cover letter is a document sent with a résumé that provides additional information on your skills and experience. Besides targeting your résumé, a cover letter is one of the best ways to prove to a potential employer that you are a good fit for the company. It's also an effective way to show a little bit of your personality and expand on items (such as an internship or volunteer experience) that you could only list on your résumé.

A cover letter is effective if it explains both the reasons for your interest in the company (what you think the strong points of the company are, for example) and how your strengths, skills, and past experiences will complement and improve the organization. Exhibiting this requires tact, as you want to show that your skills will improve the company while also highlighting what you think it's already doing well. You don't want to say, "I notice you have a really ugly website, and I could help you improve it with my design skills"! Remaining positive on both sides will make employers think about what you can do for them without making them defensive. Criticizing your prospective employer in any way will also come across as disrespectful. At the very least, a cover letter should express a high level of interest and knowledge about the position.

If you are sending your résumé through the mail, the cover letter will be a separate sheet of paper that's put in the envelope on top of the résumé. Keep it to one page. If you're sending your résumé via email, the résumé will likely

TRUE OR FALSE?
ARE YOU A COVER LETTER
AND RÉSUMÉ EXPERT?

1. Job seekers do not use cover letters anymore.
   False. Cover letters are often requested by employers, and they give you a good way to present a bit of your personality and facts or achievements that you could not easily include on your résumé.
2. A résumé should ideally be one page.
   True. You don't want to overwhelm the hiring manager with information, just facts that will help you to get the job.
3. You should use as many different fonts and design elements as possible on your résumé so that you will impress the hiring manager with your creativity.
   False. Simple and straightforward is best on your résumé. Your accomplishments, not your résumé design, should impress the hiring manager (unless you're in a creative field; in that instance, a little extra visual flair to your résumé is fine).

be an attachment, while the cover letter is in the body of the email. The cover letter is one more opportunity for you to communicate respect and maturity. It is also a good place to convey a little bit of your personality or other information that is hard to include in a résumé. For example, you can use your cover letter to show your enthusiasm for working at the company or in the particular job. If you're applying for a job at an environmental organization such as the Sierra Club, you could reference (in just a sentence or two) your membership in the organization and your pleasure that the organization recently reached some of its conservation goals. Organizations seek to hire motivated people who want to be in that particular job. Showing enthusiasm may be just the thing that gets you noticed.

The bottom line: Do not miss this chance to prove to a potential employer that you are well suited for and enthusiastic about the position.

RESEARCH PROJECT

Create a résumé that summarizes your educational and work experience as well as your skills. Then create a cover letter for a real or imaginary job. Show these documents to your parents or school counselor to receive feedback. Update these documents as you move through life and gain more experience.

TEXT-DEPENDENT QUESTIONS

1. What should you not include on a résumé?
2. What are three main résumé formats?
3. Why is a cover letter a useful job application tool?

accommodating: willing to fit in someone else's wishes in a helpful way

approachability: how easy you are to talk to and do business with

portfolio: a collection of your best work (writing, designs, photos, etc.) that you show to an employer during a job interview

salutation: a greeting

CHAPTER 4

INTERVIEW ETIQUETTE

ACING THE INTERVIEW

For entry-level positions at chain stores, you may be able to land a job just by filling out an application—but things are not so simple when it comes to finding a career. A career is more than just a job; it is the course of work you will be taking up for a long period of time, sometimes your entire life. A potential employer is very aware of this, which makes their hiring choices all the more important. This is going to be a long-term relationship! Imagine if you were about to invite someone into your family. You would want to know more about them than just what a single piece of paper could tell you. You'd want to talk to them to learn more. You'd want to interview them.

A job interview is a meeting with someone at a company who will be in control of whether or not you get hired. It is where you will discuss, face-to-face (or sometimes via video interview), your qualifications for a job. When applying for a career, an effective résumé will be able to get you an interview—and that is the place where your etiquette, manners, and personality will be most important!

TRUE OR FALSE?
ARE YOU AN INTERVIEW EXPERT?

1. It's ok to wear blue jeans to an interview.
2. Presenting proper body language is very important during the interview.
3. You should always send a written thank-you note after the interview.

Test yourself as you read. See the end of this chapter for True or False answers.

FIRST IMPRESSIONS

An employer spends only about thirty seconds looking at a résumé, and it takes a similar amount of time (between thirty seconds and four minutes) for an employer to begin to form an opinion of a potential employee. The first few minutes of an interview create what is known as a first impression, and you don't want to miss this chance to begin to form the image of yourself that you want to leave in the mind of your interviewer.

If an employer wants to interview you, they'll probably either call or email you to set up a time. If a prospective employer calls, make sure to use good phone etiquette. Say, "Hello, this is [your name] speaking," when you answer (don't say, "Yo!"), and speak slowly and clearly. If you answer by email, make sure you proofread your writing, begin with a salutation, and sign your full name.

If you are unavailable during the time when a potential employer asks you to come in for an interview, inform them of this and ask if there are any other times that are convenient. Attempt to be as accommodating as possible. Since you are applying to help a company, being accommodating communicates that you will be helpful once you have been hired. So be careful about saying

At the beginning of your interview, it's important to greet the interviewers in a friendly, confident manner; introduce yourself to and shake hands with each member of the interview team; and maintain good body language.

you're unavailable. If you have a doctor's appointment, that's one thing—but if you planned to hang out with a friend, you should probably ask your friend to reschedule rather than miss this opportunity to land a job.

It's a good idea to assess how much time it will take you to get to the interview so that you do not have any surprises because of bad weather, traffic accidents, or road construction. Many job seekers actually travel from their home to the interview site a few days before the actual interview so that they can get the "lay of the land" regarding parking, public transportation, etc. Also, on the day of the interview, have a backup transportation plan (bus, train, ride from friend, etc.) ready in case your car doesn't start or you encounter another bump in the road.

It's a good idea to arrive about twenty minutes before your interview. This gives you an extra cushion of time should you have any transportation issues.

Be sure to leave enough time to get to your interview in case you encounter car trouble or other transportation issues.

Use this time to catch your breath and get settled, review your notes or portfolio, or otherwise prepare.

Greet the receptionist in a friendly and respectful manner. Every action you take once you enter the building sends a message of who you are and how you treat people (remember the concepts of manners and etiquette?). Also, remember that hiring managers will sometimes ask the receptionist for their impression of you as another way to assess your personality and manners. Everything you do (whether it is positive or negative) makes a difference when you're trying to get a job.

When first meeting the interviewer, be enthusiastic and energetic. Smiling is an important sign of your personality. Would you want to invite someone into your family who wasn't happy to be part of it? Shake hands with each person who will be interviewing you, make good eye contact, and introduce yourself with your first and last name.

Do not sit down unless you are asked to do so. If you are not asked to sit immediately, politely ask your interviewer where they would like you to be seated. When sitting, plant your feet firmly on the floor, keep a straight back, and do not cross your arms or legs.

If you work in a creative area, such as fashion design, you should bring a portfolio of your best work to the interview.

Make sure to be aware of your posture. Don't slump or hunch over. Don't sprawl in the chair or put your feet up. An open, respectful posture means keeping your shoulders square with the person you are speaking to. This communicates an openness and willingness to listen.

If you are asked if you would like a drink, politely decline (you don't want to end up spilling it all over yourself or your interviewer!), and if you have brought anything with you, place it on the floor beside your seat (better yet, don't bring any food or liquids into the interview). Once sitting, your hands should be placed on your thighs. Do not fidget in your chair, and try not to use too many hand gestures. When people are nervous, they often move their hands far too much. Remember, presenting yourself is about making yourself look as natural as possible, so try not to appear nervous.

A career advisor provides five tips for interview success.

Other important things to keep in mind during your interview:

- Don't chew gum
- Turn off your phone and do not look at it during the interview
- Listen closely to the questions before answering
- Do not interrupt the hiring manager
- Have extra copies of your résumé ready in case they are requested

Your Appearance

An important part of a first impression has to do with what you wear to the interview. People show respect for an organization, individual, or event by dressing up. Dressing appropriately communicates to an employer that they matter and that you respect them and their business.

It is critical to be clean from your head to your toes. Any creative piercings, hairstyles, and tattoos should be left at home or concealed. If you wear glasses, make sure that the lenses are clean. Do not wear cologne or perfume, and check your face, teeth, and clothes before you enter the room. Fresh breath is a must, but do not chew on gum or suck on any mints. Remember that your appearance sends messages whether you want it to or not, so make sure to dress as well as you can!

Formal business attire is considered proper etiquette for any interview. For men, this includes:

- a suit that is either gray, navy, or charcoal
- a clean, pressed white shirt
- a conservative tie (visit www.artofmanliness.com/articles/how-to-tie-a-tie to learn how to tie it properly!)
- dark, over-the-calf socks that match your suit (no white athletic socks with your nice suit!)
- a black leather belt
- black leather shoes that are polished

Formal business attire for women includes:

- a dark suit (if you are wearing a suit skirt, the skirt should be knee length)
- a light-colored blouse
- polished, professional shoes (no large heels or open-toed shoes)

There is an old adage: "Dress for the career you want to have." A well-dressed person will be that much more confident and will show the respect that they have for the situation they are in. You are on a stage the moment you walk into the building where the interview will take place, so make sure that your costume is flawless!

It's ok to be nervous during an interview, but don't let your nervousness ruin your chances of landing a job. Be confident and focus on conveying your skills and accomplishments to the hiring **manager.**

Personality

No one should ever underestimate the power of people skills in an interview. If an interviewer likes you, they will hope you will do well. They will explain questions more fully, they may give you an example of an answer to a question, or they will simply become more relaxed when they pose questions and evaluate your answers. And if they're relaxed, it will be easier for you to act naturally as well!

Your personality can never take the place of being qualified for a position. However, if you have gotten this far—if you've been asked in for an interview—then you probably have some skills the employer already finds desirable. They will be interviewing other people who have similar skills. Your personality can push you to the top of the list, even if you aren't the most qualified person. The family metaphor is useful again when thinking about this. If your family supported themselves by farming, would you want to invite an excellent farmer with an unsavory personality into your family? Or would you want to invite an adequate farmer who would be willing to work hard and at the same time be someone you would enjoy spending time with?

As with your résumé, you should do your best to target your personality to the job position that you are applying for. This means you may want to highlight different aspects of your personality, depending on the job. A salesperson, for example, has to be very outgoing and sociable as well as have good powers of persuasion. For a software engineer, this does not matter as much. This doesn't mean you pretend to be someone you're not, though. If your natural personality is not really suitable for the job, then you should probably not be applying for the job in the first place!

While some personality traits may be more appropriate for some job settings than others, almost all employers value certain qualities. These include confidence, approachability, a sense of humor, trustworthiness, and leadership. As you discuss your past experiences and relevant knowledge, make sure to keep these qualities in mind—and mind your manners! Demonstrating your sense of humor in a job interview, for example, is not about cracking jokes of your own but about laughing if your interviewer makes a humorous comment (even if it is not very funny). It's also about being self-deprecating, which means having the ability to poke a little fun at yourself. The ability to laugh at yourself shows that you don't take yourself too seriously or have a big ego. It also shows that you are confident enough to make a joke at your own expense.

There is no definite formula for interview success. Just be as relaxed, friendly, and respectful as possible.

QUESTIONS TO ASK DURING THE INTERVIEW

The hiring manager may ask if you have any questions. It's a good idea to prepare a short list of questions about the company or the position before the interview (and add anything else that comes to mind during the interview). This shows that you've done your research and are very interested in getting hired. Remember: Don't ask questions that can easily be answered by reviewing the company's website or the job listing, or that were already covered in the interview. Here are a few suggestions:

- What is the work environment like?
- Can you tell me about the company culture?
- Will I be expected to work additional hours to complete projects?
- Will I have to travel for this position? If so, how much and to where?
- To whom will I report? Will I manage any workers? If so, may I meet them?
- How will my job performance be measured?
- What sort of advancement opportunities are available?
- Do you offer management training or mentoring programs for young workers?
- What information can you provide me regarding the stability of the company?
- What are the goals of the company in the next five years? Ten years?

THE END OF THE INTERVIEW

As the interview concludes, the hiring manager may explain what will happen next. For example, they might say, "Thank you for meeting with us. We plan to

It's important to end your interview in a positive way with a smile, a handshake, and a thank you for the opportunity.

interview five more candidates in the next two weeks, and then we will make a final hiring decision. We'll contact you in approximately three weeks." If they do not provide this information, it's important to ask about the next steps because you want to know what to expect and understand the company's hiring timeline. During this time, you should also continue to look for a job and participate in interviews at other potential employers.

When the interview ends, stand up, shake hands with each person who interviewed you, and thank each for the opportunity.

FIGHTING STRESS DURING THE JOB SEARCH

When you're looking for a job, the future can seem like a terribly scary time. For some people (depending on their field of work), looking for a job can become a job in and of itself. It can be stressful to have to spend your time this way.

Stress is one of the main reasons that people act out angrily or violently. It is also one of the main reasons people forget to use their manners and etiquette. If you become stressed, there are things you can do: Talk to a friend, take a walk, exercise, meditate, or pray. If necessary, see a doctor, therapist, or counselor. When you're relaxed, you will see that your manners and etiquette greatly improve. You can be your best self!

The future may seem confusing and frightening sometimes—but it's also full of new opportunities. Do your best to take advantage of them.

AFTER THE INTERVIEW

After you exit the interview, it's a good idea to head to a local café or other relaxing spot to debrief yourself. Write down what you believe went well and not so well. These notes will help you prepare for future interviews. Did the interviewer ask you a question that you could not answer or that you didn't answer very well? If so, it's not the end of the world, but you need to work on your answers to these questions for future interviews. Remember, each interview that you participate in is a form of training that helps you become a more attractive job candidate.

Saying Thank You

Following up after an interview is a great way to ensure that you're remembered. Even if you're not chosen for the position, you want to make sure that the hiring manager remembers you as positively as possible. If the company has job openings in the future, the hiring manager may remember you and give you a call. As soon as you get home, send a short thank-you email to the hiring manager. You can say something similar to the following:

Dear Mr. Smith,

It was a pleasure to meet with you to discuss the open software engineer position at your company. Thank you for the opportunity, and I look forward to hearing back from you regarding the position.

Sincerely,

Your Name and Contact Information

Follow up with a handwritten thank-you note sent via regular mail as soon as possible. In the old days, most job seekers sent a handwritten note, but this is not true today. It's smart to send such a note because it shows a personal touch that may help you to stand out from other candidates. You can also use this note to reiterate your interest in the job and, most importantly, clean up

ARE THANK-YOU LETTERS IMPORTANT?

The answer is yes! Eighty percent of human resources managers who were surveyed by the staffing firm Accountemps in 2017 said that they took thank-you messages into account when deciding whom to hire. Although thank-you notes remain an important application credential, the same survey found that only 24 percent of job applicants sent a thank-you note—a 27 percent decrease from 2007. The bottom line: Always send a thank-you note.

any poor responses to interview questions and/or add new information that may help you land the job. Keep the note short and positive.

If someone you know helped you get the interview, make sure to thank them for helping you, even if you didn't get the job. Building a strong network is one of the best ways to increase your chances of success in the future. The more people who know you and like you, the more job opportunities will likely come your way.

And how do you get more people to like you? By presenting yourself as best you can—with good manners, good etiquette, and respect—in each and every situation you find yourself. You never know what could lead to a job!

VIDEO INTERVIEWS

A growing number of employers are conducting job interviews by using Skype, FaceTime, Google Hangouts, or other software. They're doing so because it saves time and allows them to interview a wider range of candidates (such as those who live in other cities or even other countries).

Some employers conduct these interviews live, while others use an online system that asks applicants to record themselves answering a series of questions. Regardless of whether your interview is live or recorded, it's important to prepare for this special format because it is much different than meeting in person. Here are some tips to follow to have a successful video interview:

- **Treat the video interview as if it's being done in person.** You should prepare the same way and dress professionally—from head to toe.
- **Think carefully as you dress for the interview.** Some clothing styles and colors work better than others on video. Various shades of blue

(navy, sapphire blue, sky blue, etc.) often look better on video than red, white, or other colors. Be careful if you wear black because it can create dark shadows on your face. Pinstripe, chevron, plaid, and houndstooth patterns on clothing often do not look good on video. Stick with solid colors.

- **Test your technology ahead of time to make sure your camera and microphone work correctly.** Download the video software at least a few days before the interview and do a test run with a friend or family

Video interviews are increasingly being used by companies, nonprofits, and other organizations to screen and interview job applicants.

member. That way, you can check the video and sound quality, your body language, lighting, etc.

- **Create a professional setting for your interview.** Make sure there is appropriate lighting, but don't set up too close to a window because you might get an unwelcome glare. Get rid of clutter that will appear behind you on the video, and try to set up a quiet space where you will not be disturbed by barking dogs or other household noise.

- **Look at the camera.** This sounds kind of obvious, but a video interview can go awry if your external camera is not aligned with your face (if it's not, you'll be looking up or down, and it will make you look weird). Be sure to make "eye contact" by looking into the camera, not at the person's image on the bottom of the screen.

TRUE OR FALSE?
ARE YOU AN INTERVIEW EXPERT?

1. It's ok to wear blue jeans to an interview.
   False. Always wear a business suit to an interview to send a message that you are professional and take the interview seriously.
2. Presenting proper body language is very important during the interview.
   True. If you slouch, yawn frequently, or fail to make eye contact, the interviewer may think that you're bored and uninterested in the job.
3. You should always send a written thank-you note after the interview.
   True. It shows that you appreciate the opportunity to interview, allows you to reiterate your interest in the job, and gives you the chance to "clean up" answers to questions that you believe you did not answer well during the interview.

- **Anticipate technical issues.** A strong internet connection can easily go bad in a matter of seconds, so it's a good idea to prepare a backup plan. At the beginning of the interview, exchange telephone numbers with the hiring manager so that you can continue if your internet connection dies. This sends a message that you are detail-oriented and organized.

PRACTICE MAKES PERFECT

Interviewing skills, like all skills, need to be practiced. Maybe you were so nervous at your last interview that you froze and couldn't think of any answers to the questions posed to you. Don't let it get you down. Think of it as a learning experience. Next time, you'll know what to expect and you won't be as nervous.

RESEARCH PROJECT

Participate in a mock interview with a family member or friend. Ask them to tell you what you did right and wrong during the interview, and work to improve any areas where you were deficient.

TEXT-DEPENDENT QUESTIONS

1. How should you dress for a job interview?
2. Can you name three questions that you should ask during an interview?
3. Can you provide three ways to prepare for a successful video interview?

colleague: a coworker

flustered: stressed, confused, and anxious

human resources department: the unit of a company or other organization that is responsible for payroll, benefits, hiring, firing, addressing worker complaints, and staying up to date with tax laws

CHAPTER 5

YOUR FIRST DAY ON THE JOB

JOB SEARCH SUCCESS

Congratulations! You've landed your first real job. Take some time to celebrate, but then you need to get to work preparing for your first day on the job. It's normal to be a little nervous. You'll be required to learn new skills and do new tasks. There will be all types of new people to meet and get to know. You'll have to learn the location of your boss's office and the break room, washroom, copy room, and other important office spots. But don't get too nervous, because tens of millions of people start their first jobs each year and most are successful.

GETTING READY FOR WORK

Your first day on the job is one of the most important days of your career. Think about this first day like the first ten minutes of a job interview. Everything that

TRUE OR FALSE?
ARE YOU READY FOR YOUR FIRST DAY?

1. Now that you've got the job, you don't need to worry about manners and etiquette.
2. It's extremely important to make a good impression on your first day of work.
3. You should wait a few weeks to introduce yourself to your coworkers.

Test yourself as you read. See the end of this chapter for True or False answers.

you say or do—good and bad—will create an impression with your boss and coworkers that will be hard to shake. If you make a good impression, life will be a lot easier and, with time and hard work, you'll get promoted and receive a pay raise. If you fail to follow instructions, are unfriendly to the receptionist, or don't refill the coffeemaker when you drink the last cup, you'll have to work hard to change people's perceptions of you. And you can forget about getting a raise or promotion until you change that bad impression to a good one.

Learn what to do during your first ninety days on the job.

It's important to perform well on your first day whether you're a surgical technologist or an entry-level office worker.

SEVEN THINGS TO DO ON YOUR FIRST DAY OF WORK

There are many things you should do on your first day on the job. Here are some important steps to take to ace the first day of what is hopefully a long and successful career.

Dress for success. It's important to dress professionally whether you're a clerk or a company president. Doing so sends a message that you take your job seriously. It can also put you in a professional mind-set from day one. If you find on your first day that your coworkers dress a bit more casually (business casual instead of suits and ties), you can loosen up your look as the week progresses. Remember: It's better to be overdressed than underdressed in most life situations.

Arrive to work early. Get there at least fifteen minutes early so you're not flustered or even late if you get stuck in traffic, your train is delayed, or another problem arises. Do this for at least the first few weeks so that you avoid being late for work.

Meet your boss and coworkers. Check in with your boss to let them know that you've arrived. They may ask you to meet with a member of the human resources department to fill out employment forms, or they may just put

It's important to meet as many of your coworkers as possible on your first day.

If you are friendly and hardworking in your first weeks on the job, you'll quickly become a key member of your work team.

you to work. Introduce yourself to your coworkers. Try to remember people's names and their job duties. You may need their help as you navigate your new workplace. Doing so also shows that you are friendly and confident. It's ok to be nervous, but you'll find that most people are friendly to new workers. They've been there before and want you to succeed.

Be enthusiastic and energetic. Don't be football-game or rock- or rap-concert enthusiastic and energetic, but speak clearly, with energy, and at a good volume; demonstrate positive body language (sitting up straight, no slouching as you walk the halls, good eye contact, etc.); and be willing to take on any job, big or small.

Learn the layout of your office. Find the locations of the elevator, copy room, etc. so that you can do your work efficiently. Know where you can go and not go. The last thing you want to do is accidentally wander into the CEO's office during a big meeting.

Get to work. Start impressing your boss and coworkers by going right to work. If you run out of work to do and your boss is busy, read the employee or department manual, meet some more coworkers, or become more familiar with the layout of the office. Also, keep your breaks short, and stay fifteen or so minutes late each day to show that you are committed to the job.

Be yourself. Don't try to impress your boss or coworkers by bragging or acting overconfident. Just simply be the best version of yourself that's possible, and you'll go from new employee to trusted colleague in no time.

TRUE OR FALSE?
ARE YOU READY FOR YOUR FIRST DAY?

1. Now that you've got the job, you don't need to worry about manners and etiquette.
   False. Good manners and proper etiquette are important throughout your life, both in your personal and professional relationships.
2. It's extremely important to make a good impression on your first day of work.
   True. First impressions stay in the minds of your coworkers for a long time. That's why it's important to be respectful, focused, friendly, and hardworking on your first day at work and beyond.
3. You should wait a few weeks to introduce yourself to your coworkers.
   False. Doing so may send a message that you're aloof (snobby) or lack confidence.

RESEARCH PROJECT

What are three of your fears (e.g., being late for work, no one liking you, etc.) about your first day on the job? What can you do to address these issues before you start your job? Write a 250-word report that analyzes each fear and presents strategies to address them.

TEXT-DEPENDENT QUESTIONS

1. Why is it important to make a good first impression at work?
2. How should you dress on your first day?
3. How early should you arrive on your first day?

SERIES GLOSSARY
OF KEY TERMS

accreditation: The process of being evaluated and approved by a governing body as providing excellent coursework, products, or services. Quality college and university educational programs are accredited.

application materials: Items, such as a cover letter, resume, and letters of recommendation, that one provides to employers when applying for a job or an internship.

apprenticeship: A formal training program that combines classroom instruction and supervised practical experience. Apprentices are paid a salary that increases as they obtain experience.

associate's degree: A degree that requires a two-year course of study after high school.

bachelor's degree: A degree that requires a four-year course of study after high school.

certificate: A credential that shows a person has completed specialized education, passed a test, and met other requirements to qualify for work in a career or industry. College certificate programs typically last six months to a year.

certification: A credential that one earns by passing a test and meeting other requirements. Certified workers have a better chance of landing a job than those who are not certified. They also often earn higher salaries than those who are not certified.

community college: A private or public two-year college that awards certificates and associates degrees.

consultant: An experienced professional who is self-employed and provides expertise about a particular subject.

cover letter: A one-page letter in which a job seeker summarizes their educational and professional background, skills, and achievements, as well as states their interest in a job.

doctoral degree: A degree that is awarded to an individual who completes two or three additional years of education after earning a master's degree. It is also known as a **doctorate**.

for-profit business: One that seeks to earn money for its owners.

fringe benefits: A payment or non-financial benefit that is given to a worker in addition to salary. These consist of cash bonuses for good work, paid vacations and sick days, and health and life insurance.

information interview: The process of interviewing a person about their career, whether in person, by phone, online, or by email.

internship: A paid or unpaid learning opportunity in which a student works at a business to obtain experience for anywhere from a few weeks to a year.

job interview: A phone, internet, or in-person meeting in which a job applicant presents their credentials to a hiring manager.

job shadowing: The process of following a worker around while they do their job, with the goal of learning more about a particular career and building one's network.

licensing: Official permission that is granted by a government agency to a person in a particular field (nursing, engineering, etc.) to practice in their profession. Licensing requirements typically involve meeting educational and experience requirements, and sometimes passing a test.

master's degree: A two-year, graduate-level degree that is earned after a student first completes a four-year bachelor's degree.

mentor: An experienced professional who provides advice to a student or inexperienced worker (mentee) regarding personal and career development.

minimum wage: The minimum amount that a worker can be paid by law.

nonprofit organization: A group that uses any profits it generates to advance its stated goals (protecting the environment, helping the homeless, etc.). It is not a corporation or other for-profit business.

professional association: An organization that is founded by a group of people who have the same career (engineers, professional hackers, scientists, etc.) or who work in the same industry (information technology, health care, etc.).

professional network: Friends, family, coworkers, former teachers, and others who can help you find a job.

recruiting firm: A company that matches job seekers with job openings.

registered apprenticeship: A program that meets standards of fairness, safety, and training established by the U.S. government or local governments.

resume: A formal summary of one's educational and work experience that is submitted to a potential employer.

salary: Money one receives for doing work.

scholarship: Money that is awarded to students to pay for college and other types of education; it does not have to be paid back.

self-employed: Working for oneself as a small business owner, rather than for a corporation or other employer. Self-employed people must generate their own income and provide their own fringe benefits (such as health insurance).

soft skills: Personal abilities that people need to develop to be successful on the job—communication, work ethic, teamwork, decision-making, positivity, time management, flexibility, problem-solving, critical thinking, conflict resolution, and other skills and traits.

technical college: A public or private college that offers two- or four-year programs in practical subjects, such as the trades, information technology, applied sciences, agriculture, and engineering.

union: An organization that seeks to gain better wages, benefits, and working conditions for its members. Also called a **labor union** or **trade union**.

work-life balance: A healthy balance of time spent on the job and time spent with family and on leisure activities.

FURTHER READING & INTERNET RESOURCES

FURTHER READING

Christen, Carol and Richard N. Bolles. *What Color Is Your Parachute? for Teens: Discover Yourself, Design Your Future, and Plan for Your Dream Job*. 3rd ed. New York: Ten Speed Press, 2015.

Peterson's. *Teens' Guide to College & Career Planning*. 12th ed. Highlands Ranch, CO: Peterson's, 2016.

Tieger, Paul D., Barbara Barron and Kelly Tieger. *Do What You Are: Discover the Perfect Career for You Through the Secrets of Personality Type*. 5th ed. New York: Little, Brown Spark, 2014.

Trillo, Alejandro. *Vices and Virtues: Knowing, Accepting and Improving Yourself*. Liguori, MO: Liguori Publications, 2015.

Zichy, Shoya and Ann Bidou. *Career Match: Connecting Who You Are with What You'll Love to Do*. 2nd ed. New York: AMACOM Books, 2017.

INTERNET RESOURCES

www.pamf.org/preteen/growingup/etiquette.html: This resource provides etiquette advice for a variety of situations—from talking on the telephone to greeting people to table etiquette.

www.thebalancecareers.com/high-school-resume-examples-and-writing-tips-2063554: Visit this website for advice on writing a résumé if you are still in high school; sample résumés are also provided.

www.livecareer.com/career/advice/jobs/teen-job-strategies: This website from LiveCareer provides eleven interview tips for teens.

www.roberthalf.com/blog/job-interview-tips/how-to-ace-your-video-interview-for-job-seekers: Visit this website for tips on how to ace a video interview.

EDUCATIONAL VIDEO LINKS

Chapter 1
An educator gives advice on choosing what to do after high school: http://x-qr.net/1M8s

Chapter 2
See some examples of surprising business etiquette practices around the world: http://x-qr.net/1M2n

Chapter 3
Learn six things that every high school student should put on their résumé: http://x-qr.net/1M3S

Chapter 4
A career advisor provides five tips for interview success: http://x-qr.net/1JwT

Chapter 5
Learn what to do during your first ninety days on the job: http://x-qr.net/1LQw

INDEX

AUTHOR BIOGRAPHIES

Andrew Morkes has been a writer and editor for more than twenty-five years. He is the author of more than twenty-five books about college planning and careers, including all of the titles in this series, many titles in the Careers in the Building Trades series, the *Vault Career Guide to Social Media*, and *They Teach That in College!?: A Resource Guide to More Than 100 Interesting College Majors*, which was selected as one of the best books of the year by the library journal *Voice of Youth Advocates*. He is also the author and publisher of "The Morkes Report: College and Career Planning Trends" blog.

Christie Marlowe lives in Binghamton, New York, where she works as a writer and web designer. She has a degree in literature, cares strongly about the environment, and spends three or more nights a week wailing on her Telecaster.

PHOTO CREDITS